Finding Sarah

Candice Means

BookLeaf Publishing

India | USA | UK

Finding Sarah © 2024 Candice Means

All rights reserved.

No part of this publication may be reproduced, stored in a retrieval system, or transmitted, in any form or by any means, electronic, mechanical, photocopying, recording or otherwise, without the prior written permission of the presenters.

Candice Means asserts the moral right to be identified as author of this work.

Presentation by *BookLeaf Publishing*

Web: www.bookleafpub.com

E-mail: info@bookleafpub.com

ISBN: 9789363314665

First edition 2024

I dedicate this book to all the survivors of human trafficking whom think or feel like they are all alone. You are not alone and I hope you find the courage to raise your voice in awareness and bring out the beautiful person you were created to be.

ACKNOWLEDGEMENT

God
Human Trafficking Task Forces
Refuge For Women
My 2 Beautiful Daughters Lindsay Kathryn and Audreonna Faith
Jennie Cannon
Shawna Nunn Wharton
To all the women in my life who continue to provide support, understanding, and love

PREFACE

"I survived what I survived so that I may help other's stay alive"

That feeling of being so uninvited into a world that is filled with such darkness is crippling. I was able to find the love and strength of God and I am now able to use my voice to bring awareness to the darkness that lives among us.

How Much Does She Cost,
He Said

How much does she cost, he said
Top bidder can take her to their bed

Be a good little girl and do as you are told
Since birth you have been sold

How much does she cost, he said
For another day she will dread

Will somebody find her and see her worth
Or will they continue to pass her back and forth

How much does she cost, he said
As she hangs on by a thread

When will the day come
When she no longer wants to be numb

How much does she cost, he said
As the horror in her life continued to spread

No end in sight, no hope to be found
Stuck in this cycle of trauma, she will be bound

No Hope Is To Be Seen

No where to go
No place to call home
Abused and neglected
She feels all alone

The thoughts from her past
Continue to progress
How long will this last
Is all she really asks

Fading slowly into the midst of hell
As if she is under a cruelty spell
No where to turn, No where to go
For the past has became her main bio

Enduring the cruel cycle of polytrauma
Her body remains in great cauma
No hope is to be seen
For she will always feel unclean

Why

Why didn't you save me
Why didn't you protect me
From all these bad men
Where the devil lived within

Was I a bad girl
Did I cry too much
I promise I'll be good
Why am I not enough

Tears roll down my face
No help in sight, not even a trace
Despair sets in
Am I slowly dying within

Will the day come
When the pain will end

Silent whispers

Mommy can you hear me
Daddy where are you
It's dark in this place
And I do not feel safe

The bars on these cages are so cold
Almost as cold as the bad men's souls
Trapped in this life, a life of despair
How much more do I have to bear

I'm hungry mommy
I wish you would come feed me
I'm so tired daddy
I wish you could come hold me

Being alone and scared
My heart breaks and tears
Trapped in this life
Where no one seems to care

God where are you, are you even there
For this life I have been given, I was not
prepared
Will the day come when someone will say
Come here my child, I will keep you safe

A Trapped Soul

Trapped in a world full of hatred and chaos
A little girl sits wishing it would all just stop
As the night sky darkens and her dreams come
to a halt
Her worst fear begins to creep down the hall

As each step he takes
Her soul begins to fill with hate
How can a man be so strong
Feel so powerful with her innocent soul

Her eyes begin to see no light,
For his rage brought upon her
Has caused no hope to be in sight
Everything around her becomes a blur

The darkness within him
Begins to rattle her cage
Be a good little girl
As his aggression begins to hurl

Silent Goodbyes

Nightly screams run through the house
As I sit in my cage quiet as a mouse
Knowing that they will come
This time I hope it's only one

Tears roll down my face
Curling up into a small embrace
Be still and don't make a sound
Please God, Help me be found

The cold air from the winter nights
It seems as though I am completely out of sight
No one can hear my muted cries
For they have become my silent goodbyes

As the night set in and the demons appear
The damage to come is surly unclear
No more scream are heard at night
For they grew their wings and have took flight

Contrite

Bruised and Broken
The darkness devours all her emotions
Trapped in a world
Full of treacherous hurls
When will the day come
Where she will be fully numb

She roams this world always in terror
Wondering how much more she will have to
bare
You will never find another soul like hers
For she my dear will never be yours

Her soul is covered by the one true God
For she has even beat the odds
You tried to destroy her and take her soul
Yet only God is in control

So as you bid your farewells goodbye
Just know my God is truly the all high
For my soul is surly not to die

Can You Hear Me

God can you hear me
When the devils prepare to fight
God can you hear me
On these lonely cold nights
God can you hear me
As I grip my legs close and hold myself tight
God can you hear me
As my soul shakes with fright
God can you hear me
As I pray to see your light
God can you hear me
I'm ready to come home, I'm ready to reunite
God can you hear me
When I cry all night
God can you hear me
For I am ready for my home flight

Lost

Where has she gone
Why can she not be found
Whom has she become
For they say she has become more than some

Dissociated Episodes cause her to switch
As if she has a horrible twitch
We have Princess and Sarah along with Chris
and James
All before the age of 6 they came
Wait here comes Candice and Tabitha
Surly they got this

As the memories and trauma continue to
progress
We have no choice but to be suppressed
Here comes Skylar
The one who will defend and protect
She is extremely direct
And in unsafe situations she will detect

For I know this is all hard to comprehend
Trust us, we want this all to end
For this is not fair, not one single ounce
Yet we refuse to give in, we refuse to renounce

For the judgement and ridicule is okay
It's something you never have to go through, I
pray
Innocence and trust was taken at a young age
Switching into alters is what made us okay

One day we will heal and become so strong
Yet until then
Sarah must be gone

Trust and safety are big keys in our life
Through only then can we surly revive

Whom Have You Become

Darkness surrounds her chaotic mind
Running through life as if she was blind
Not a care in the world if she was to die
All she wants is to run and hide

Thoughts of suicide flow through her soul
She is slowly losing all control
How much longer can she hold on
For her life is almost gone

One more drink, she is surly to pass
The tears fill her eyes as she takes her last gasp
Begging and pleading, she yells at God
She will not be the one to beat the odds

She hits her knees one last time
For her strength is too weak for this climb
To climb this road of despair
There's not much more that she can bare

She has become someone she hates
For a world full of darkness is what they create
The sadness she holds on the inside
She can no longer hide

Courageous

Be strong they say
Try to get through just today
One day at a time, this too shall pass
When the world on my shoulders feels like a big
mass

It's time to grow up and let go of the past
Yet, how can this be possible when PTSD will
always last
Work through your trauma, you can do it they
say
Surely God will make a way

Walk the path of those you follow
Don't allow your demons to make you feel
hollow
Just get over it and let it go
How can you say this, when you don't even
know

You are so strong and brave
All you need to do is pray
Pray to what, I surely do ask
Because everything and everyone just wears a
mask

You must trust someone or something
Yet all I want to feel is nothing
Falling into the midst of numbing
Has my life become nearly nothing

Finding Sarah

Too young to fight back
Too weak to scream for help
She had no choice
Other than to become someone else

Dissociated Episodes was her only escape
Kinda like she wore her own superwoman cape
The trauma was too much for her to bare
There were many alters she would have to wear

See the mind is a powerful asset
For she had created her own cachette
Escaping reality was her new norm
For her life had always been a huge storm

She Is

She is not for the weak
For she has survived more than she speaks
Crawled up from the pits of hell
What was sent to kill her, did not prevail

She is stronger than she will ever believe
Because this world has beaten her down to her
knees
Begging and crying she has screamed
Help me Lord, God help me please

For the love she has for God, no one can
compare
Because HE saved her life when no one else
cared
They all turned their heads
As the monsters ripped her to threads

You see, she is not for the weak
For now she has the courage to speak
Sitting in silence is no longer her call
For as long as she has God on her side
You are surly to befall

Lost And Alone

Fingertips cover her mouth as she screams
Depression at an all time high it seems
Night terrors and sweats fill her bed at night
For there's not a flicker of light in sight

How long will this one last
How long will the demons harass
Trapped in the cycle of pain
She hides from everyone and doesn't complain

What would happen if someone saw her tears
Would they comfort her or just give blank stares
How quickly would they shut her down
Act as if she was only a clown

You are supposed to be so strong
How dare you cry and not prolong
Prolong the healing
Prolong the pain
For no person is here for the haul

Go on and close your eyes at night
For only the darkness will come to light
Lost and alone in a world so cold
She longs for the day she is called home

Never Again

Breaking the chains of childhood trafficking
Grasped her soul as if she is panicking
Trauma is all that she knew
And throughout her life it only grew
Memories of the horrific nights
Flood her brain as if hell ignites

Come over here and be a good little girl
Do as you are told and no one will get hurt
These are the words she heard so often
How much does she cost even as an orphan

Born into a world full of greed
It was as if she came with a nifty deed
Highest buyers come take your pick
I have a cute little girl who knows how to trick

She will do as she is told or else
Or her back will see the lashes of these belts
You can cry and scream all that you want
For the lashes will continue from the back to the
front

So be a good little girl and do as your told
For you are to be sold

Rescued and brought to Kentucky
She truly is so very lucky
For what she survived
She will never forget
Yet her pricetag says
Never Again

Despair

A soul lost in despair
Nothing in this world could compare
The darkness I was born into
No one knew exactly what I would go through

Trapped in the midst of hell
No one to care, no one to tell
Loud screams became small whisper
Please don't hurt me, I promise I will be good,
mister

Ripping and tearing of my soul
I was left without a single ounce of control
The damage within my soul was too much to
bare
As they continued to grab me by my hair

Do as we say and as you are told
This basement floor sir, it is so cold
You are hurting me sir, please let me go
I don't want to do this, I don't want to show

Put on this dress and be a good little girl
Go on and give them a little twirl
Like the auctioneer at a car show
You shall be sold, you shall go

Forgotten

How is it possible to become someone else
How was it possible to be born into such a mess
Trapped in a cage beaten and starving
Was this the curse of an hereditary marking

Locks and chains surround my ankles
Chain to the darkness surrounded by wrangles
Trapped within the pits of hell
As if my soul was born to sell

God where are you, can you hear my cries
Can you see the darkness within their eyes
Why are they so mean, can you not see
Will the day come when I will be set free

How can they be so cruel and evil
I want to be set free, just like your eagles
How could you allow this to happen
For they say God, that you have compassion

Can you see the pain in my soul
I am broken and will never be whole
You could have stopped them, you could have
saved me
Yet God, you did not set me free

Trapped with the memories and the night terrors
Do you even keep track of my tears
Am I a lost soul, just to be forgotten
As humanity keeps on trotting

Forgotten in a world so cruel
Yet God, did you not compare me to a jewel
Cherished and loved, that's what you said
Yet many days I wish I was just dead

They Come Out At Night

Tears slowly roll down her face
No help in sight, not even a trace

She grips her knees with a secure brace
As the shadows of darkness creeps in on her face

She closes her eyes as they get closer
She wonders how long until it is over

Be a good little girl you can hear them whisper
As she cringes and says I promise I will mister

I won't cry, I won't shed any more tears
For the darkness around her, there is no more
fear

Her soul darkens as the light begins to fade
She is there to pay the price that once was made

This is a debt you surely owe
For you life shall be tossed below

Slaved to all those around her
She was lost in a world where no one could find
her

There were no more tears and no more fight
For she began to know when the demons came
out at night

Piece By Piece

Piece by piece she is slowly losing herself
A pain she hopes no one will ever feel
themselves
She's a strong one they surely do say
As the darkness lingers and continues to play

How much longer can she hold on
As she hopes the pain will pass on
She grips the sides of her thighs
The darkness surrounds her as she closes her
eyes

Secret prayers she sends to God
As the demons continue to poke and prod
A fight between Heaven and hell
A life of darkness she wishes to never tell

Begging and Pleading she cries out in pain
Just stop these memories within my brain
Save me from these horrific nights
For what they are doing to me just isn't right

The Battle For Her Soul

A battle for her soul was sure to exist
As if she was on the devils hit list
A darkness so cruel and so unbelievably evil
Tossing her innocence into an upheaval

Will the day come where she will see light again
Maybe a day where such darkness can't possibly
live within
Used and abused by the devil himself
She was used for the pride of themselves

As if a trophy that sat high on a shelf
Only those could obtain her if they had wealth
No one could understand the true breadth
For soon they would surely be put to death

Hold on my dear daughter, I hear the whisper
For my Savior has come as the great ripper
A child so innocent and so pure
How could the devil use her soul as a lure

Tugging and pulling, the battle began
For God himself, HE is the one
No longer slaved to all of these men
Her soul was set free

From the evil that she lived within

Her life was not easy, her life was not fair
Yet she continues to bow down in prayer
For the devil has lost the battle I say
Vengeance is the Lord's, and they shall pay

Stop Childhood Human Trafficking

Their silent cries scream out for help
No one can hear their innocence yelps
As the world turns their backs
The traffickers continue on their attacks

Neighbors pretend like they don't know
They just continue on with the flow
Society pretends as if it doesn't exist
And humanity continues to just dismiss

Dismissing the signs in front of their eyes
As if it is nothing but a bunch of lies
Human Trafficking is on the rise
Wearing their mask is a powerful disguise

Would you cry out for help
If it was your child who had yelped
Would you search high and low
Or would you continue to just watch the show

Trapped in the cycle of dismissal
As our children are attacked by their missiles
Darkness surrounds our children as the
traffickers ripple

Seeking to destroy anyone they can cripple

Will you continue to sit back and watch
Or are you ready to stand up and march
Raise your voice for those innocent souls
Save our children from these evil trolls

www.ingramcontent.com/pod-product-compliance
Lightning Source LLC
LaVergne TN
LVHW010949200726
843509LV00013B/2337